THE
COMING
ECONOMIC
FLOOD

THE
COMING
ECONOMIC
FLOOD

ANTHONY HO

CREATION
HOUSE

THE COMING ECONOMIC FLOOD by Anthony Ho
Published by Creation House
A Charisma Media Company
600 Rinehart Road
Lake Mary, Florida 32746
www.charismamedia.com

Unless otherwise noted, all Scripture quotations are from the Holy Bible, New International Version of the Bible. Copyright © 1973, 1978, 1984, 2011 by Biblica, Inc. Used by permission.

Scripture quotations marked ESV are from the Holy Bible, English Standard Version, Copyright © 2001 by Crossway Bibles, a division of Good News Publishers. Used by permission.

Design Director: Justin Evans
Cover design by Nathan Morgan

Visit the author's website: www.jcmanifesto.org

Library of Congress Cataloging-in-Publication Data:
2014910977
International Standard Book Number: 978-1-62136-789-5
E-book International Standard Book Number:
978-1-62136-790-1

While the author has made every effort to provide accurate telephone numbers and Internet addresses at the time of publication, neither the publisher nor the author assumes any responsibility for errors or for changes that occur after publication.

First edition

14 15 16 17 18 — 987654321
Printed in Canada

DEDICATION

*This book is first and foremost dedicated
to my beloved Lord and Savior, Jesus
Christ, who pulled me out of the road to
destruction into life in Him. All honor
and glory to Him for all eternity!*

*It is also dedicated to my beloved and
my joy, my wife, Annie, and my three
children, Alvan, Alayna, and Asher, whose
constant support I need so much as we
simplify our lives together; and to my
beloved friends who have encouraged
and supported my ministry in one way
or another, especially Patrick Tan Kin
Way, Gary Yong, Chang Peng Soon, Peter
Goh, and the late Paul Vincent Wan.*

CONTENTS

PREFACE

Brothers and sisters, think of what you were when you were called. Not many of you were wise by human standards; not many were influential; not many were of noble birth. But God chose the foolish things of the world to shame the wise; God chose the weak things of the world to shame the strong. God chose the lowly things of this world and the despised things—and the things that are not—to nullify the things that are, so that no one may boast before him.

—1 CORINTHIANS 1:26–29

AFTER A DECADE in full-time Christian ministry, I have come to realize that godliness can be manipulated by charlatans as a means of financial gain, fame, and power. The sudden emergence of so many false teachers who adulterate the gospel for the sake of gain is surely a sign of the beginning of the birth pains spoken of by our Lord Jesus. Bizarre signs and wonders are common experiences reported every day. The prophetic ministry foretelling the future in general or the future of individual believers is also flourishing.

With such a backdrop, I am very reluctant to write on my own experience of visions and the message God had given me that happened quite some time ago for two reasons. First, they sound so incredible and, second, I am not a product of the mainstream factory producing Christian ministers, and so I believe the message will not be well received. I do not wish to be perceived as just another charlatan trying to make something incredible out of my ministry. All these years of ministry and traveling in the

Asian region from Singapore have been funded entirely through unsolicited love gifts and personal savings by the grace of God. If I must boast, I rather boast in my weakness.

God continued to speak to me that, should I not share the message, blood would be on my hands. Whether the message is incredible and not well received should be the least of my concerns. I have been obedient to share the message in regional pastoral conferences to which God has so miraculously led me in recent years. Should I not be obedient to write a book on the message, which will be more detailed than what I would normally share within an hour or so with churches during conferences and worship services?

God has His way of encouraging me through His Word. He reminded me that it is faithfulness that matters, not my ability to do the job. Not my credentials. Not the size of the job. And He deliberately chooses those who are not wise by worldly standards so that none can boast in His presence. He deliberately chooses the weak to shame the strong.[1]

Having read of similar visions and insights from American pastors like Jonathan Cahn and John Hagee in their respective books *The Harbinger* and *Four Blood Moons*, it is a timely encouragement from them that I should share of my similar message demonstrating God's revelation given to people in the East as well as in the West.

The message I am sharing is a message of God's coming judgment.

It is my prayer that the book will make us see that God's coming judgment is an act of mercy, and we must repent in response to His mercy. Our sins of being over-fed, of arrogance, prosperous ease, and indifference to helping the poor have heaped up so high to heaven today.[2] These root sins of Sodom are already breeding a great harvest of bad fruit of homosexual sin and lawlessness, seen through the violent atrocities happening around the world. God can either abandon us to continue in our self-centered and degrading way, as we desire, and be lost forever, or He can will an impending judgment and warn us to repent, which is an act of mercy.[3] We should humble ourselves before God, seek His face, and turn from these sins of self-indulgence right away.[4] We should seek His wisdom diligently to make the right preparation to face it.

Noah, being divinely warned of things not yet seen and moved with godly fear, prepared an ark to save his family while others continued to eat, drink, and make merry.[5] We are now living as in the days of Noah.[6] If we prepare like Noah, we are none the poorer if the judgment never comes. If the judgment really comes and we are totally unprepared, we will suffer much emotionally and physically. We will experience the plagues of His judgment: mourning, famine, and death.[7]

The following article from OregonFaithReport.com on the high suicide rates among Protestants pretty sums up the urgent need for emotional preparation to face the possibility of unemployment or other hardship.

> According to Dr. Harvey Brenner at John Hopkins University, for every one percent increase in the unemployment rate [in the United States], an additional 1,200 people can be expected to commit suicide. And the Christian community is not exempt. ReligiousTolerance.org reports that among faith groups in the United States, Protestants—despite their stand against suicide—have the highest suicide rate.
>
> "That's tragic and yet understandable," confirms

Laura Baker, executive director of Prasso Ministries. "Many people who have been in church all their lives still have their faith knocked out from under them due to job or financial loss brought on by the recession."[8]

Chapter 1
THE FIRST VISION

But when he, the Spirit of truth, comes, he will
guide you into all the truth. He will not speak
on his own; he will speak only what he hears,
and he will tell you what is yet to come.

—JOHN 16:13

SEPTEMBER 3, 2001

I WAS AT THE airport in Singapore leaving for New York City for the usual quarterly global sales meeting. I worked for Nu Horizons Electronics Corp., a global distributor of electronic components listed on NASDAQ, as the chief executive of their Far East subsidiaries. (Nu Horizons Electronics Corp was acquired by Arrow Electronics Inc. in 2010.)[1] It would be a twenty-four-hour flight from Singapore to Newark Airport via Dubai. Unlike previous meetings, which I attended only with my sales director for Asia, I decided to bring along all the Asian managers for this meeting. We had a great financial year, and I wanted to reward them for their hard work.

Actually, the Far East subsidiaries of Nu Horizons Electronic Corp. were joint ventures between Nu Horizons and myself. I started an enterprise to represent electronic component manufacturers in Southeast Asia in 1993. By 1997, due to the Asian financial crisis, I had to seek new partnership with American manufacturers. I secured an order fulfillment partnership with Nu Horizons and her subsidiaries, NIC Components Corp. and Titan Logistics

Inc. in Asia. In 1999, I proposed a joint venture, as the sales in Asia were getting substantial, and the joint venture subsidiaries were eventually established in late 1999.

We had our quarterly sales meeting from September 4 through September 7 at the headquarters of Nu Horizons Electronics Corp. in Melville, Long Island. As usual, after days of long and hard sessions of discussion stretching from nine o'clock in the morning till after dinner in the evening, we would rest and relax in Manhattan over the weekend after the meeting proper had ended.

It would be a wonderful time of rest and relaxation. The first-timers to New York would get a chance to sight-see Manhattan, the Statue of Liberty, and the natural history museum. In the evening, we would dine in the best restaurants and watch the Broadway shows.

SEPTEMBER 7, 2001

We checked into a hotel just next to the World Trade Center on the afternoon of September 7. After a nice steak dinner, we went to a Broadway show before settling in a jazz bar to relax for the whole evening. We retired late to the hotel.

SEPTEMBER 8, 2001

After breakfast we went our separate ways. The manager in charge of the Taiwan market had a close friend working in Manhattan, and she wanted to meet up with her. The rest of our group went shopping. There was a factory outlet for past-season Hugo Boss suits just across the street from where we stayed.

I joined the group interested in going shopping. In the late afternoon, we were at a café on the ground level of the World Trade Center. The rest joined us at this café later.

These managers were with me at this café: the manager responsible for the Singapore market; the sales director for Asia; the sales manager of another enterprise of mine; and the female manager responsible for the Taiwan market. The managers for Hong Kong and China had left for home. Since the morning of September 8 I had this premonition that there would be a terrorist attack on the city. As we chatted at the café and I shared my premonition, I told them not to go up to the observatory deck of World Trade Center in case the terror attack happened there.

These managers of mine hardly read such news, and they were not aware of the earlier bomb attack on the World Trade Center in 1993. According to certain reports, the attack was meant for the United Nations Building, but the security was too tight there. I told them the plot of the American action/thriller movie *Peacemaker* starring George Cooney and Nicole Kidman, for conversation's sake. It was about the revenge of a Yugoslav who somehow believed the United Nations to be ultimately responsible for the Yugoslav wars in which his wife and children were killed. He managed to smuggle the small nuclear bomb into New York when he travelled as a member of a Bosnian diplomatic delegation.

The more I talked about the terror attack, the more uneasy my managers felt. I even shared about taking certain measures, should we see a truck driving down the street at high speed. We could run across to the Century 21 building. And if possible, we should stay in structures that could withstand the collapse of buildings or in the open. By this time, I had this firm premonition of the collapse of the World Trade Center buildings.

We did not usually bring along any camera on our trips. But on this trip my female manager had a camera. I guessed she wanted to take some pictures with her close friend. My other enterprise manager remarked in jest that we should take some pictures with the World Trade Center in the background in case they really collapsed in the event of a terror attack. He lay on the ground and took pictures of us standing with the World Trade Center in the background. By lying down on the ground, he could capture the whole World Trade Center buildings in the pictures.

In the evening we went to the wedding dinner reception of one of our colleagues from the United States who was the regional sales manager for the eastern region of the US. It was held in a restaurant on the fourth level of a building near the beach facing the World Trade Center. I was really getting nervous by then that the attack was imminent. While sipping a cocktail and standing in the balcony facing the World Trade Center, I saw the vision of planes laden with bombs attacking the World Trade Center! I knew then that it was not going to be a truck laden with bombs but planes!

SEPTEMBER 9, 2001

After the wedding reception I went straight back to the hotel, as I was feeling really uneasy about the vision. I prayed. I could not sleep. At 3:00 a.m., I called up my secretary to reconfirm all the airline tickets of everyone in our group. It was 3:00 p.m. Singapore time.

I booked the wake-up call for everyone. We left for the airport in the morning after breakfast. It was not a pleasant thing for me to send everyone back home at such short notice. I believe my managers would have liked to spend one or two more days in Manhattan.

We arrived back in Singapore in the late evening of September 10.

SEPTEMBER 11, 2001

I got into the office at 9:00 a.m., and to my surprise, my staff had organized a birthday party for me. It was my birthday. Later in the evening I was with my wife in a café nearby my home. At about 10:00 or 11:00 p.m., my mother called. She asked if I was still in New York. She was explaining some breaking news on TV. I could not figure out what she was trying to tell me. When we went back home and switched on the TV to watch CNN News, we saw the startling news! What did God want to tell me?

So many people died in this terror attack. Close to three thousand people died.

We might not have been caught inside the World Trade Center during the attack, had we stayed back in Manhattan instead of heading for home. First, we would usually have breakfast at nine o'clock, and the earliest we would be shopping in the World Trade Center was in the afternoon. We were more likely to check out museums in the morning if we had the time. Second, we had made up our mind not to go to the observatory deck of the World Trade Center.

So what was God trying to tell me?

As an engineer by profession in the early years of my career, statistics and probability were something we worked with every day. We designed experiments and implemented control systems based on the probability of the outcome deduced from the statistical data received from the experiments. I knew it would be too much of a coincidence for my vision of the attack to happen to occur right before the actual attack, considering the odds of all the following events occurring altogether: I had the vision just a few days before the actual event; I was at the exact place of the vision; I had a vision of the actual terror attack using planes—which was unprecedented—and on the World Trade Center (and not the United Nations Building); and it occurred on my birthday. The probability of all these events occurring will be so miniscule as to be mere coincidence.

I was sure God was giving me a message.

Over the next few days I read in the newspapers of the close encounters of several fellow Singapore citizens. Any close encounter would be newsworthy. I was tempted to share with the press about my vision. My managers could testify to what I would say about the vision. I was still dazed by what had happened. Several questions ran through my mind, which eventually deterred me: What purpose would it serve? Would I be promoting myself as one with special gifts? Sharing a testimony to further the kingdom of God was the last thing on my mind then, even though I was sure God had given me a message.

I was a Sunday Christian all along ever since I was baptized in the seventies. I had all the wonderful trappings of a jet-set executive. I was admired for my professional success. I was making very good money. In the society of Singapore then, I was every mother's dream. I studied in the best secondary school, the best polytechnic academy, and finally in the top local university, graduating with honors in electrical and electronics engineering. I was offered one of the most prestigious post-graduate scholarships, which I turned down. And now, I was a successful corporate man in just fifteen years!

Surely Christ was not sending me a message to give up everything and follow Him.

The vision was a turning point for me. I knew the probability of having that precise vision at the precise time was simply too slim to be pure chance. The conviction of the Holy Spirit every day gave me no peace to continue in the corporate life with all the excesses anymore.

In late 2002 I resigned and sold all the equity of my subsidiaries back to the parent company. I began to seek God
and read the Scriptures religiously. I knew the parable of
the rich fool by heart all along, yet I failed to see that I had
been that rich fool all along.[2] Though I had given much to
the poor and charity in the past, the main preoccupation
in my mind was constantly how to build bigger barns in
which to store all the bountiful harvest coming and telling
my heart to relax and indulge in dissipation.

From 2003 to 2005 I spent most of my time meditating
on the Word of God and praying. God's Spirit showed me
through His Word how I had wasted my life so far. I did
nothing close to the manifesto of Christ in sharing the
gospel, giving sight to the blind, setting the captives fee,
and relieving the oppressed.[3] I was just like the five foolish
virgins not eagerly awaiting the return of the Bridegroom.[4]
I thought I was a disciple of Christ. But everything—my
family, myself, and my possessions—had a tighter hold over
me than did the things of the kingdom of God.[5]

I married at a young age, but my first son came seven
years later, in 1994. I had two more children in 2003 and
2004 by the grace of God. They were miraculous answers to
our prayers. My wife was suffering from endometriosis and
was advised by her gynecologist to be pregnant again in
order to be fully cured of that condition. She had an earlier
operation to remove the cyst, but it grew back again. She
was already thirty-eight, and pregnancy risks were height-
ened. However, the female gynecologist was both famous
and a Christian. She encouraged us to try the in-vitro fer-
tilization (IVF) program.

I reluctantly agreed to the IVF program, though I knew
in my heart it would not work. I told her that God would
answer my prayer instead of going through that program, if

God so willed. (I was not disputing the fact that God could answer the prayer of childless couples through the IVF program, but I discerned it would not be the case for us. We had this trust in God.) We did the intracytoplasmic sperm injection (ICSI) procedure twice considering our near hopeless condition, but to no avail. My eldest son and I prayed fervently for my wife's healing, and God did heal her when she was pregnant again—naturally! Praise and thanks be to God!

Though my wife's medical condition and the arrival of two more children somehow consumed much of my attention, the blessings of God answering my prayer cemented my faith in God, and He was definitely getting my whole attention.

The vision had such an impact on me and made me reflect seriously on the purpose of life. The conviction of the Holy Spirit made me realize I was not born again. I did not have a new heart and a new spirit in me to deny myself, take my cross daily, and follow Jesus as Lord of my life.[6] Giving up the corporate life with all the excesses was the first step toward a new life in Christ. The diligent study of Scripture and the guidance of God's Spirit helped me to truly find the way, the truth, and the life in Christ.[7]

I continued to pray fervently for revelation from God about the specific message of the vision. It became a bit clearer when I had the second vision in 2005.

Chapter 2

THE BEGINNING OF THE BIRTH PAINS

*As Jesus was sitting on the Mount of Olives, the disciples come to him privately. "Tell us," they said, "when will this happen, and what will be the sign of your coming and of the end of the age?" Jesus answered: "Watch out that no one deceives you. For many will come in my name, claiming, 'I am the Messiah,' and will deceive many. You will hear of wars and rumors of wars, but see to it that you are not alarmed. Such things must happen, but the end is still to come. Nation will rise against nation, and kingdom against kingdom. There will be famines and earthquakes in various places. **All these are the beginning of birth pains.** Then you will be handed over to be persecuted and put to death, and you will be hated by all nations because of me. At that time many will turn away from the faith and will betray and hate each other, and many false prophets will appear and deceive many people. Because of the increase of wickedness, the love of most will grow cold, but the one who stands firm to the end will be saved. And this gospel of the kingdom will be preached in the whole world as a testimony to all nations, and then the end will come.*

—MATTHEW 24:3–14, EMPHASIS ADDED

ID THE MESSAGE that I was sure God was telling me through the vision have something to do with judgment? Some pastors in America believed the terror attack was a wake-up call to the erosion of values in a Christian society. I do not want to delve into this potential cause because some three thousand died in this sad incident, and many were fine people. Or is it a warning of a bigger catastrophe to come?

Since the seventies we have been taught by some doomsday prophets that the return of Jesus is coming soon. They pointed to the return of the Jews to their homeland in Israel in 1948 and the use of Hebrew as the official national language as proof that the end-time prophecies would be fulfilled in earnest after these events. Some believed Jesus would return in 1988, which would be one generation from 1948, in fulfillment of the prophetic word of Jesus in Luke 21:32. Some believed the Cold War would lead to World War III. Yet others believed the Y2K phenomenon, also known as the Millennium Bug, would cause a global financial collapse and set off a chain of events leading to the formation of a world government.

Meanwhile, globalization, which refers to the emergence of an international network of social and economic systems, took off in the mid-eighties. By the mid-nineties four main movements of trade, capital and investment, migration, and the dissemination of knowledge were greatly enabled by technological advances in transportation and telecommunications, especially the Internet.

With globalization came easy access to consumer goods and growing prosperity, stoking the flames of materialism, which became the main preoccupation of global citizens. Christians are not exempt. We know that anything fascinating us more than God is sinful and is displeasing to God. So as to absolve guilt in pursuing our materialistic dreams, many false teachers came on to the scene to teach false gospels such as the prosperity gospel, hyper grace gospel, and several variants of the same message touting wealth-and-health desires. All of a sudden, the faithful gospel of being born again—from the Protestant Reformation in the sixteenth century to the 1970s in the twenty-first century—was greatly adulterated to justify the materialistic dreams of many professing Christians.

We were taught in the true gospel that no one can enter the kingdom of God unless we are born of water and of the Spirit. We must die to our sin and be born again with God cleansing our sin and giving us a new heart and a new spirit.[1] The only way God can work in us is that we must trust and believe in Jesus as our Savior and Lord who died for our sin once and for all.[2] His blood will cleanse away our sin once and for all, and His Spirit will live in us to sanctify us to be like Him. Living as new creation in Christ, we are already dead to sin, and God's Spirit will move us to keep His commandments.[3] These false gospels do not require us to die to sin by taking our cross daily and following Jesus.

It dawned on me that one of the signs mentioned by Jesus in Matthew 24 was the appearance of many false prophets and teachers.

> As he sat on the Mount of Olives, the disciples came to him privately, saying, "Tell us, when will these things be, and what will be the sign of your coming and of the end of the age?" And Jesus answered them, "See that no one leads you astray. For many will come in my name, saying, 'I am the Christ,' and they will lead many astray. And you will hear of wars and rumors of wars. See that you are not alarmed, for this must take place, but the end is not yet. For nation will rise against nation, and kingdom against kingdom, and there will be famines and earthquakes in various places. All these are but the beginning of the birth pains. Then they will deliver you up to tribulation and put you to death, and you will be hated by all nations

for my name's sake. And then many will fall away and betray one another and hate one another. And many false prophets will arise and lead many astray. And because lawlessness will be increased, the love of many will grow cold. But the one who endures to the end will be saved. And this gospel of the kingdom will be proclaimed throughout the whole world as a testimony to all nations, and then the end will come.

—MATTHEW 24:3–14, ESV

From the above verses, Jesus mentioned the following signs, which will precede His coming:

- False Christs;

- Wars and rumors of wars;

- Famines;

- Earthquakes;

- Persecution, leading to many falling away;

- Many false prophets, leading many astray;

- Lawlessness will increase;

- The love of many will grow cold.

Yet all these signs are merely the beginning of the birth pains.

Throughout the history of the last two thousand years or more since Jesus ascended to heaven, such signs have been observed anyway. So how can we be certain that right now we are staring at the beginning of the birth pains? Are we really living in the last period of the last days? Many pastors and theologians believe we are because of the exponential increase of these signs, which differentiate the chaotic times from the stable times. Can exponentially increased instances of these signs be considered conclusive proof? In childbirth, at the onset of labor, pain caused by uterine contractions will intensify until the baby is born. The intensification of birth pain is a good illustration of the sudden escalation or exponential occurrence of calamitous events.

As an electronics engineer by profession early in my career, I have observed the intrinsic behavior of the bathtub curve. We have used the bathtub curve to predict the time required for an accelerated aging process to weed out weak parts being produced in the manufacturing line. This initial time phase is known as the infant mortality phase. Then comes the stable phase of the life of the product. Eventually comes the wear-out phase. We use such predictability to work out the mean time to failure of the manufactured products. Human mortality also mirrors this bathtub curve. There is reason to believe as we observe the exponential increase of global events like depletion of critical resources and population growth in the wear-out phase that the end outcome will be catastrophic.

Dr. Albert A. Bartlett has contributed significantly to the study of physics. According to his Web site, he was "professor emeritus in nuclear physics at the University of Colorado at Boulder. He was president of the American Association of Physics Teachers in 1978, and in 1981 he received their *Robert A. Millikan Award* for his outstanding scholarly contributions to physics education."[4] In his seminal presentation "Arithmetic, Population and Energy," he mentioned this famous phrase: "The greatest shortcoming of the human race is the inability to understand the exponential function."[5]

I believe Dr. Bartlett said so because we are predictably irrational when we face a mathematical fact, like the exponential function. We are likely to fail to understand why we suddenly face bottlenecks in many situations when we fail to appreciate that steady, modest growth in a particular situation, though at a small percentage, can suddenly result in doubling the outcome of a situation.

In his lecture, he was trying to explain that within a finite system, modest annual growth at a certain percentage cannot continue indefinitely. In the example of oil usage, the human race may be caught unawares when modest annual growth of the use of critical resources like oil due to population growth can result in sudden escalation of depletion in a relatively short period of time. The logic is simple and irrefutable. And when this critical stage of depletion of oil happens, for example, we will face an apocalypse.

I like this particular illustration given by Dr. Chris Martenson in Chapter 4 of his presentation, *The Crash Course*, which is based loosely on Dr. Bartlett's famous lecture.

The purpose of this mini-presentation is to help you understand the power of compounding. If something, such as a population, oil demand, a money supply, or anything, steadily increases in size in some proportion to its current size, and you graph it over time, the graph will look like a hockey stick.

Said more simply, if something is increasing over time on a percentage basis, it is growing exponentially.

Using an example drawn from a magnificent paper by Dr. Albert Bartlett, let me illustrate the power of compounding for you.

Suppose I had a magic eye dropper and I placed a single drop of water in the middle of your left hand.

The magic part is that this drop of water is going to double in size every minute.

At first nothing seems to be happening, but by the end of a minute, that tiny drop is now the size of two tiny drops.

After another minute, you now have a little pool of water that is slightly smaller in diameter than a dime sitting in your hand.

After six minutes, you have a blob of water that would fill a thimble.

Now suppose we take our magic eye dropper to Fenway Park, and, right at 12:00 p.m. in the afternoon, we place a magic drop way down there on the pitcher's mound.

To make this really interesting, suppose that the park is watertight and that you are handcuffed to one of the very highest bleacher seats.

My question to you is, "How long do you have to escape from the handcuffs?" When would it be completely filled? In days? Weeks? Months? Years? How long would that take?

I'll give you a few seconds to think about it.

The answer is, you have until 12:49 on that same day to figure out how you are going to get out of those handcuffs. In less than 50 minutes, our modest little drop of water has managed to completely fill Fenway Park.

Now let me ask you this—at what time of the day would Fenway Park still be 93 percent empty space, and how many of you would realize the severity of your predicament?

Any guesses? The answer is 12:45. If you were squirming in your bleacher seat waiting for help to arrive, by the time the field is covered with less than

5 feet of water, you would now have less than 4 minutes left to get free.
And that, right there, illustrates one of the key features of compound growth...the one thing I want you take away from all this. With exponential functions, the action really only heats up in the last few moments.
We sat in our seats for 45 minutes and nothing much seemed to be happening, and then in four minutes—bang!—the whole place was full.[6]

So, the sudden escalation part in the exponential curve is the critical phase to watch in any event.
Are we seeing this critical phase in the emergence of many false prophets on the scene?
Are we seeing this phase in the occurrence of many earthquakes measuring a Richter scale of 8 and above in these few decades, as compared to other centuries?
Are we seeing this phase in the number of wars and rumors of wars?
Are we seeing this phase in the size and frequency of famines?
Are we seeing this phase for all these occurrences altogether?
I believe we have reason to be concerned, as we are indeed seeing the exponential behavior of all these signs right now.
Our Lord Jesus had mentioned the word *suddenly* several times. We are warned often not to be caught unawares when He returns again.

Therefore stay awake—for you do not know when the master of the house will come, in the evening, or at midnight, or when the rooster crows, or in the morning—lest he come suddenly and find you asleep. And what I say to you I say to all: Stay awake.

—MARK 13:35–37, ESV

But watch yourselves lest your hearts be weighed down with dissipation and drunkenness and cares of this life, and that day come upon you suddenly like a trap. For it will come upon all who dwell on the face of the whole earth.

—LUKE 21:34–35, ESV

While people are saying, "Peace and safety," destruction will come on them *suddenly*, as labor pains on a pregnant woman, and they will not escape.

—1 THESSALONIANS 5:3, EMPHASIS ADDED

Whoever remains stiff-necked after many rebukes will *suddenly* be destroyed—without remedy.

—PROVERBS 29:1, EMPHASIS ADDED

Many will still be caught unawares in the day of our Lord. The suddenness of the day of our Lord coming upon us seems to mirror the suddenness of the escalation of an event in an exponential situation.

Just as it was in the days of Noah, so will it be in the days of the Son of Man. They were eating and drinking and marrying and being given in marriage, until the day when Noah entered the ark, and the flood came and destroyed them all. Likewise, just as it was in the days of Lot—they were eating and drinking, buying and selling, planting and building, but on the day when Lot went out from Sodom, fire and sulfur rained from heaven and destroyed them all—so will it be on the day when the Son of Man is revealed.

—LUKE 17:26–30, ESV

It will be predictably irrational that even when the signs and their mathematical certainty are there for any event, many will still be caught unawares. It is a psychological state called normalcy bias that most have. This state causes people to underestimate the possibility of an impending disaster and the severity of its consequences. They assume the event will not happen, as it has never happened before. People in this state tend to downplay the signs and infer a less severe outcome.

Of course, there are also some people who overreact. They will cry wolf every time some signs are evident. Both are extremes to be avoided.

In the article "The Normalcy Bias and Bible Prophecy" by Todd Strandberg, he writes:

> One of the most tragic examples of the normalcy bias is the experience of the Jews in Nazi Germany. Barton Biggs, in his book, *Wealth, War and Wisdom*, gave a very good description of what happened:
>
> > By the end of 1935, 100,000 Jews had left Germany, but 450,000 [remained]. Wealthy Jewish families...kept thinking and hoping that the worst was over.
> >
> > Many of the German Jews, brilliant, cultured, and cosmopolitan as they were, were too complacent. They had been in Germany so long and were so well established, they simply couldn't believe there was going to be a crisis that would endanger them. They were too comfortable. They believed the Nazis' anti-Semitism was an episodic event and that Hitler's bark was worse than his bite. [They] reacted sluggishly to the rise of Hitler for completely understandable but tragically erroneous reasons. Events moved much faster than they could imagine.[7]

Chapter 3

THE SECOND VISION

*After this I saw another angel coming down from heaven. He had great authority, and the earth was illuminated by his splendor. With a mighty voice he shouted: "Fallen! Fallen is Babylon the Great!...For all the nations have drunk the maddening wine of her adulteries. The kings of the earth committed adultery with her, and the merchants of the earth grew rich from her excessive luxuries.... When **the kings of the earth** who committed adultery with her and shared her luxury see the smoke of her burning, they will weep and mourn over her.... **The merchants** who sold these things and gained their wealth from her will stand far off, terrified at her torment. They will weep and mourn and cry out: 'Woe! Woe to you, great city, dressed in fine linen, purple and scarlet, and glittering with gold, precious stones and pearls! In one hour such great wealth has been brought to ruin!' Every sea captain, and all who travel by ship, the sailors, and all who earn their living from the sea, will stand far off. When they see the smoke of her burning, they will exclaim, 'Was there ever a city like this great city?' They will throw dust on their heads, and with weeping and mourning cry out."*

—Revelation 18:1–3, 9, 15–19, emphasis added

B ESIDES MY DAILY devotion and diligent study of theology ever since receiving the first vision, I was also studying the end-time prophecies to see if there was any possibility, however remote, that the vision of 9/11 was one of the signs of any of these prophecies.

Then in late 2004 I had the second vision of the collapse of the global financial system. Whether it was terms like *financial perfect storm, financial firestorm, financial earthquake,* or *financial tsunami* that kept flashing in my mind; a vision or dream of a repeat of the violent riots in Indonesia; or stories of hardship in Thailand, the Philippines, Malaysia, and other Asian nations in the 1997 Asian financial crisis, my mind was troubled all the time. The premonition of a global financial system collapse grew stronger and stronger in my devotional time over several months that I eventually blogged about this second vision in an Asian Web site on June 20, 2005, and titled it "The Coming Financial Tsunami" to warn fellow Christians to be financially prudent.[1] I wrote that the Americans were beginning to behave like the Asians in the developed Asian countries, obsessed with residential assets. They were beginning to learn that they could draw out cash from their properties through refinancing to pay for the instant gratification of luxuries like cars and big holidays. To compound the problem further, the US banks were giving subprime loans with no down payment, which even the Asian banks did not provide in earnest prior to the 1997 Asian flu. By June 2005, I saw the reckless lending of US banks to consumers to purchase homes easily, which would cause much hardship in the near future when the housing bubble burst. I was certain that the financial system collapse would be caused by the bursting of the housing bubble in the United States.

At that time when I had this vision, I had little or no knowledge of economics, the monetary system, the banking system, and the financial health of the economies of the major trading partners in the world. I do not know how fiat currency comes into existence. Why can sovereign countries print their own money? Why are some worth more than others? How are the economies of individual countries being run?

I began to read every evening to better understand how the housing bubble bursting could precipitate this collapse. I wondered, What does this collapse mean in terms of human suffering, like loss of jobs and destruction of wealth? It would be a good three years before the 2008 financial crisis. I named this crisis "the financial tsunami" after the massive tsunami on December 26, 2004, which killed more than two hundred thousand people in India, Thailand, Indonesia, and many small islands in the Indian Ocean. *How could I know that the cause would be the bursting of the US housing bubble, which was just in its infancy stage in mid-2005?* The economists only started talking seriously about this housing bubble in 2007. Interestingly, the 2008 crisis came to be known as the global financial tsunami.

The only judgment by God on wealth on a global basis is mentioned in Revelation 18. As I read this chapter, I noticed that Babylon mentioned in Revelation 17 is different from the Babylon mentioned in chapter 18. One is judged by the Beast, while the other's wealth is destroyed by God. One is talking about a religious system, while the other describes a political cum financial system.

> After this I saw another angel coming down from heaven, having great authority, and the earth was made bright with his glory. And he called out with a mighty voice, "Fallen, fallen is Babylon the great! She has become a dwelling place for demons, a haunt for every unclean spirit, a haunt for every unclean bird, a haunt for every unclean and detestable beast. For all nations have drunk the wine of the passion of her sexual immorality, and the kings of the earth have committed immorality with her, and the merchants of the earth

have grown rich from the power of her luxurious living."
Then I heard another voice from heaven saying, "Come
out of her, my people, lest you take part in her sins, lest
you share in her plagues; for her sins are heaped high
as heaven, and God has remembered her iniquities. Pay
her back as she herself has paid back others, and repay
her double for her deeds; mix a double portion for her
in the cup she mixed. As she glorified herself and lived
in luxury, so give her a like measure of torment and
mourning, since in her heart she says, 'I sit as a queen,
I am no widow, and mourning I shall never see.' For
this reason her plagues will come in a single day, death
and mourning and famine, and she will be burned up
with fire; for mighty is the Lord God who has judged
her." And the kings of the earth, who committed sexual
immorality and lived in luxury with her, will weep and
wail over her when they see the smoke of her burning.
They will stand far off, in fear of her torment, and say,
"Alas! Alas! You great city, you mighty city, Babylon!
For in a single hour your judgment has come." And the
merchants of the earth weep and mourn for her, since
no one buys their cargo anymore, cargo of gold, silver,
jewels, pearls, fine linen, purple cloth, silk, scarlet cloth,
all kinds of scented wood, all kinds of articles of ivory,
all kinds of articles of costly wood, bronze, iron and
marble, cinnamon, spice, incense, myrrh, frankincense,
wine, oil, fine flour, wheat, cattle and sheep, horses and
chariots, and slaves, that is, human souls. "The fruit for
which your soul longed has gone from you, and all your
delicacies and your splendors are lost to you, never to
be found again!" The merchants of these wares, who
gained wealth from her, will stand far off, in fear of her
torment, weeping and mourning aloud, "Alas, alas, for
the great city that was clothed in fine linen, in purple
and scarlet, adorned with gold, with jewels, and with

pearls! For in a single hour all this wealth has been laid waste." And all shipmasters and seafaring men, sailors and all whose trade is on the sea, stood far off and cried out as they saw the smoke of her burning, "What city was like the great city?" And they threw dust on their heads as they wept and mourned, crying out, "Alas, alas, for the great city where all who had ships at sea grew rich by her wealth! For in a single hour she has been laid waste. Rejoice over her, O heaven, and you saints and apostles and prophets, for God has given judgment for you against her!" Then a mighty angel took up a stone like a great millstone and threw it into the sea, saying, "So will Babylon the great city be thrown down with violence, and will be found no more; and the sound of harpists and musicians, of flute players and trumpeters, will be heard in you no more, and a craftsman of any craft will be found in you no more, and the sound of the mill will be heard in you no more, and the light of a lamp will shine in you no more, and the voice of bridegroom and bride will be heard in you no more, for your merchants were the great ones of the earth, and all nations were deceived by your sorcery. And in her was found the blood of prophets and of saints, and of all who have been slain on earth."

—REVELATION 18, ESV

Babylon mentioned in the above chapter of Scripture is unmistakably the alliance of governments (kings of the Earth), multi-national companies, all small and medium enterprises (merchants), and the global shipping lines and ports (those who make a living by the sea) forming a global supply chain and financial system engaged in globalized trade. All have grown rich as a result of this alliance. This is the current capitalism we know today.

It is not a coincidence that Babylon is the birthplace of

the modern banking system. *Encyclopaedia Britannica Online* has this to say on the history of banking:

> Some authorities, relying upon a broad definition of banking that equates it with any sort of intermediation activity, trace banking as far back as ancient Mesopotamia, where temples, royal palaces, and some private houses served as storage facilities for valuable commodities such as grain, the ownership of which could be transferred by means of written receipts. There are records of loans by the temples of Babylon as early as 2000 BCE; temples were considered especially safe depositories because, as they were sacred places watched over by gods, their contents were believed to be protected from theft. Companies of traders in ancient times provided banking services that were connected with the buying and selling of goods.[2]

The current banking system offers so many personal loans to satisfy consumers to be able to afford the desired standard of living. Such crippling debt enslaves the average modern man.

God hates this usury system, for it enslaves the people with crippling debt. When God led the Israelites out of Egypt into the Promised Land, He gave them repeated warnings about the dangers of usury, which is borrowing money or things with an interest premium. (For further reading, you can refer to Exodus 22:25; Leviticus 25:35–37; and Deuteronomy 23:19.) And He forbade it, though Israelites were allowed to lend money at interest to non-Israelites. Obviously knowing the enslaving powers of debt, God mandated regular debt-relief programs in the years of release[3] and the Jubilee Year.[4] These institutions were designed to prevent debt from overwhelming and enslaving the Israelite population.

Since my first vision of 9/11, I had been waiting upon the Lord in prayer and diligent study of the Scripture. I believed all along that God would reveal to me the message, and with this second vision, I was certain that He had called me to share a message about the coming collapse of the global financial system. As I did not graduate from any seminary, or have any leadership position in the local church, there was hardly any network to call upon to share the message. I believed God would then open the doors for me.

Before I could go on the road to share the message, I was struck with excruciating pain at the coccyx, commonly known as the tailbone, in early 2006. I could not sit down at all. If I just sat down for a moment, I would feel excruciating pain. The whole year was spent seeking specialist treatment and therapy. Yet the pain did not diminish, and I was literally standing all the time while being awake. The specialists told me that the wear and tear of my tailbone came much too early, and there was no surgery to rectify it at that time. I have learned to pray for all circumstances, and prayer in this instance was not only my first option but also the only option. I learned to bear with the pain as time went by. I believed God would heal me, as I still had a message to share. He answered my prayer one year later. I was completely healed of the pain. Hallelujah! All thanks and praise to God and Christ, my Lord!

Soon God led me to know two senior pastors from Guangzhou and Shenyang through an alumnus brother who was serving as a missionary in Hong Kong and Shenzhen. They were overseeing a few dozen house churches with some few thousand members in these cities and were part of an alliance of thousands of churches across China with a Baptist background. They invited me to come and share in their churches in China. In late 2007 I made it to share in a pastoral conference in a village in a small town situated some one hundred and fifty kilometers from Shenyang. That was to be my first missionary trip. About one hundred and fifty pastors and ministry workers attended. As the churches were unregistered, that conference was considered to be illegal.

In the last evening of the conference I shared the prophetic word that the financial crisis would happen just after the China Olympics in September 2008.

The interest rates for the bulk of subprime loans were expected to reset in early 2008 because these loans were offered with very low teaser rates for only three years from early 2005 in earnest. I was certain the United States government would not expect a 3- to 4-trillion-dollar hole as a result of the housing bubble burst, and so she would not make the drastic decision of huge quantitative easing as an immediate remedy since it was unprecedented.

During this period from early 2008 till after the crisis blew up in September 2008, I saved up all love gifts and personal savings in order to give to these churches in need. At the same time, I was praying and looking for like-minded brothers who could also be given the same vision. I got to know two brothers from the Chinese Christian Fellowship Singapore who eventually formed a local church with me to worship and serve together in early 2009.

Meanwhile, we traveled to dispense the money to needy churches in China while waiting on the Lord for further assignment.

When 2010 came and went, I knew this financial tsunami was not the judgment mentioned in Revelation 18, as the global economy seemed to recover. Yet, I was sure that the collapse had to come in order for the one-world government to come into power as a result of the chaos caused by many worthless fiat currencies, which I will share in later chapters.

In 2011, God opened doors for me in a big way to share

in the regional mission movements. It was nothing short of the miraculous.

One evening in early 2011 a brother brought an Indonesian businessman to my home. I took the opportunity to share about my visions and the coming financial collapse. He was so intrigued that he invited me to share in the church pastored by his younger brother in Batam, Indonesia. I readily agreed.

On March 10, 2011, I went to Batam to share in a prayer meeting. Some one thousand people attended that evening. And, to my surprise, a radio crew was present to record my message.

I shared generally about the general signs of the end times, and showed charts of the exponential numerical increase of earthquakes, famine, and pestilences in the last few decades as compared to the last few centuries. I did not share about my vision of the coming financial system collapse right away in this local church. I wanted to go easy this first time, and if God were willing, I would share it in the near future.

I learned later that the senior pastor of this church, Pastor Jhonston Silitonga, is the chairman of the Body of Christ Fellowship, which is an alliance of some one thousand churches belonging to more than sixty denominations across Indonesia.

As I was sitting in a café lounge waiting for my ferry ride back home from Batam the next day on March 11, 2011, I saw the breaking news on TV of a tsunami that had just happened in Japan. For a moment we thought the TV report was about the tsunami that had happened in Aceh in 2004.

Over the next seven days, with my sermon being played on air to an audience estimated to be a million listeners, the sermon—with the mention of signs such as exponential increase of earthquakes and calamities—captured the attention of the churches in this denomination. I was subsequently invited to share in several pastoral conferences across several cities in Indonesia.

Two weeks later, a Filipino pastor, Pastor Martin Faoilan, walked into our Sunday worship service. We thought that he walked into the wrong church, as there was another Filipino worship service in the same premises. He told us that he felt led by God to attend our service. I was preaching that day. We met again on Monday to explain my mission, which is to share about the coming financial system collapse. He invited me to share with his church in the Philippines.

Two months later I travelled to the Baptist church in Villasis, Bangasinan Province. I did not know it was actually a pastoral conference, or rather, it was a conference to commission chaplains. As the leaders of this chaplaincy, the National Auxiliary Chaplaincy of Philippines (NACPHIL), are mainly Baptist or Methodist ministers, they invited mostly evangelical pastors to serve as chaplains in the Philippine government.

NACPHIL is a non-governmental organization whose purpose is to carry out the mandate of the Executive Order 173 of the Philippine government. The mandate is to "[strengthen] the authority of the Presidential Council on Values Formation towards Effective Pursuit of a Just and Moral Philippine Society. It is aimed at eradicate from all sectors the culture of graft and corruption, patronage politics, apathy, passivity...factionalism, and the lack of patriotism...to be replaced with the love of country, honest public service, integrity, honesty, and good work ethics."[5]

NACPHIL entered into a memorandum of understanding with the Ministry of Interior and Local Government on April 25, 2011. As of today, NACPHIL has commissioned some few thousand chaplains and deployed to some sixty provinces.

Chapter 4
THE MANIFESTO OF CHRIST

*The Spirit of the Lord is on me, because he has anointed
me to proclaim good news to the poor. He has sent me
to proclaim freedom for the prisoners and recovery
of sight for the blind, to set the oppressed free.*

—Luke 4:18

*Seek the LORD, all you humble of the land, who do his
just commands; seek righteousness; seek humility; perhaps
you may be hidden on the day of the anger of the LORD.*

—Zephaniah 2:3, esv

FOR THE WHOLE of 2012 I prayed and discussed much
with the leaders of these regional movements on how
to be prepared to face this coming financial system
collapse.

Not knowing exactly how we should be prepared for this
collapse, at least the revealed will of God for each one of
us is clear. We should follow the same manifesto of Christ
our Lord in sharing the gospel in word and in deed. We are
exhorted by the Word of God to spur one another toward
love and good deeds, not giving up meeting together but
encouraging one another, and all the more as we see the
day of our Lord drawing near.

In the formation of the local church with a few fellow
workers with the same vision in 2009, I have adopted the
vision and mission of the church to be based on the manifesto of Christ spelled out in Luke 4:18, which is to share the
gospel to the poor, giving sight to the blind, setting free the
captives, and relieving the oppressed. It became clear to me

that we should witness for Christ both in word and in deed as the best way to be prepared. We are to share the good news with the poor and to serve them according to their needs.

In the past century, Christians took responsibility to take social action in establishing utopia on Earth through politics and social spheres. As a result, it created a lot of distrust. Unlike social action, social *service* is about good works, serving the felt needs of the community and not correcting the root cause of the needs.

> Social activity can be a bridge to evangelism. It can break down prejudice and suspicion, open closed doors, and gain a hearing for the Gospel. Jesus himself sometimes performed works of mercy before proclaiming the Good News of the kingdom.[1]

Thus, evangelism and social service, like conjoined twins, are inseparable in our obedience to proclaim the gospel, as was the mission of Jesus our Lord, stated in Luke 4:18.

I have observed many local churches in Asia have already been involved in one or more programs in meeting needs in such categories as education, child care, nutrition, healthcare, food production, and job creation.

After much prayer, we narrowed down to three basic needs that are urgent today in most poor communities. They are cheap, clean water, cheap electricity, and equipment for farming.

I went to study the time-tested, slow sand water filtration method at the Laos water authority in Vientiane. The cost of six hundred United States dollars for one such biosand filter is too expensive and will be out of reach for most communities. I managed to import a few such biosand water filters from a Canadian NGO, Triple Quest Inc., for sixty dollars each.[2] We did a trial in a village in Batam, Indonesia, and it was a success. Indonesia has more than seventeen thousand islands. Many are inhabited with some few hundred people. By installing a biosand filter in each island, the Christian missionary is able to share this filter with all the inhabitants and gain a hearing of the gospel later.

In October 2013, the typhoon Haiyan devastated several places in the Philippines. Nearly two million people were left homeless and without electricity. We sent over some four hundred and twenty solar lamps to the disaster area in Tacloban through the National Auxiliary Chaplaincy of Philippines. The lamps proved to be so useful, as there would not be any electricity installed for the next six months due to lack of relief funds from the Philippine government.

Many parts of Indonesia do not have connection to the electricity grid. By giving the village head in each village a solar lamp, we were able to gain a hearing of the gospel later in the village.

Since 2009, we had been ministering to several villages in Java on a separate mission, and we had one hundred and five baptised members. We provided financial assistance to start some cottage enterprises, such as rearing goats and making boxes for the fishermen to wrap the fish. The church was named Kinarti Fellowship. In June 2013, the church was persecuted, and most of the members were scattered. A mob of a few hundred came to their houses. Some left earlier when threats were issued. Others were arrested by the local police to protect them from the mob.

Just four days before the persecution, the Spirit of God prompted me to have a conference with the leaders in a hotel in Jakarta instead of the city near their villages. Usually, I would pray and plan for the messages four weeks in advance. But for this last conference I had absolutely no idea of the message to share. On the very first day of the conference, I shared the word on Luke 21 about the coming persecution expected of us in the last days. In the afternoon we had discussion on how to face the persecution. It could not have been more timely to prepare them ahead! At this point of writing, we have only been able to contact the missionary who acted as our translator these four years in Indonesia.

In an experiment on an island, we purchased land and cultivated rice. We also purchased a rice mill to share with all the inhabitants for a certain percentage of their harvest. This programme helped the local church to reach out to the unsaved population on the island.

In my opinion, these three programs of meeting basic needs are the most cost effective in reaching communities and gaining a hearing of the gospel with ease if mission budget is a constraint. For the price of a biosand filter of sixty American dollars, we can provide clean water for some few hundred people. For the price of a solar lamp of fifteen dollars, we can provide light in the evening for a household. And with the rice mill and tractor costing five thousand dollars, the whole community of a few thousand people can benefit so much from it and be self-sufficient.

Chapter 5

THE GLOBAL FINANCIAL
SYSTEM COLLAPSE

For still the vision awaits its appointed time; it has-
tens to the end—it will not lie. If it seems slow, wait
for it; it will surely come; it will not delay.

—HABAKKUK **2:3**, ESV

FTER THE SECOND vision in 2005 I began to study
anything pertaining to the global economy. When
God opened doors for me to share in regional movements, my message was mainly about the coming collapse
of the global financial system.

I believed the collapse would be precipitated by either one
of these two events: the eventual collapse of the current fiat
currency system due to the uncontrollable spiraling increase
of sovereign debt of major economies like the United States,
the Eurozone, Japan, and even China and their subsequent
implosion; and the sudden exponential depletion of critical
resources, such as oil. Even the depletion of water and food
production will exacerbate the depletion of oil. New sources of
water require energy to make, such as desalination or the recy-
cling treatment of wastewater. Food production is declining
fast due to the erosion of fertile land caused by the damming
of rivers. Huge production of fertilizers is necessary to make
up for the loss of fertile land, and that depletes energy as well.

The total sovereign debt of these major trading economies is
growing very fast due to years of lack of financial prudence in
government spending and giving out generous social welfare
entitlements. The debt in these countries, like Japan and most

European countries, is so crippling today that a large portion of the income goes to pay for the interest on this debt. The social welfare entitlements are also growing fast as the population of these countries age. As there is no end in sight to the growing total debt and the growing interest payment burden, it will eventually precipitate the financial system collapse. The United States' currency was made the world's reserve currency in 1944. At that time, the United States was the largest creditor nation in the world. With a huge trade surplus with the world, she was able to invest in other countries. At that time, the US dollar was backed by gold, but that peg was removed by President Nixon in 1971.[1] Fast forward to today, when the United States has become the largest debtor nation in the world. Though official percentages give a different number, many sources say the United States' sovereign debt has just exceeded 100 percent of the GDP and is still growing.

The current balance sheet of the United States government is very telling.[2]

FINANCIAL STATEMENTS

United States Government
Statement of Operations and Changes in Net Position
for the Year Ended September 30, 2012

(In billions of dollars)	$
Revenue	
Individual income tax and tax withholdings	1925.10
Corporation income taxes	237.50
Excise taxes	81.10
Unemployment taxes	66.50
Customs duties	28.60
Estate and gift taxes	13.90
Other taxes and receipts	145.80
Miscellaneous earned revenues	19.70
Intragovernmental interest	-
Total Revenue	2518.20
Net Cost of Government Operations:	
Net cost	3814.30
Intragovernmental interest	-
Total net cost	3814.30
Intragovernmental transfers	
Unmatched transactions and balances	(20.20)
Net operating (cost)/revenue	(1,316.30)
Net position, beginning of period	(14,785.40)
Prior period adjustments–changes in accounting principles	0.70
Net operating (cost)/revenue	(1,316.30)
Net position, end of period	(16,101.00)

Any company with such year-end financial information is considered to be insolvent. Yet the United States government will continue into the future to borrow money to meet her expenses to the tune of up to five percent of her GDP. And that percentage can increase any time, should the Federal Reserve interest rates rise from the current near-zero rates when the current quantitative easing program ends. The interest payment on their outstanding debt is artificially held down by the Federal Reserve printing money and lending at near-zero interest rates at this moment.

The United States government is not alone in this irresponsible spending habit. The governments of Japan, the United Kingdom, and European nations are borrowing constantly to fund their expenses instead of bearing the pain now to deal with the runaway deficit of the budget through austerity measures to balance the budget. It cannot be done by raising taxes, as they are already at high levels. The other alternative is to spend less and bear some pain in the process. Given the current trend of low annual growth for the advanced economies, such an austerity measure will put a further damper on the growth, and no government will have the political will to do so. And even if they do, it is political suicide with slowing growth and unemployment being the collateral damage. The situation of more debt piling on huge existing debt with no end in sight will spiral to eventual collapse.

Mark Watson's Web site, *Watson's* Web, gave this comical illustration of the state of the United States economy.

> Bill and Martha together make $45,000 a year. Bill is a truck driver and Martha is a Tutor. In total their annual expenses are $133,000 a year. In order to make ends meet, they have chosen to borrow the difference on their Visa, MasterCard and Discover card. They

THE COMING ECONOMIC FLOOD

have been doing this since the crisis of 2008 when Martha got sick and could not work. Today, they have borrowed about $88,000 (annual deficit) every year to make ends meet. They now have cards with $444,000 charged on them (National debt). Next year, just the interest payments on all three cards will take up their entire check. In short, they will not even be able to service their debt, let alone pay any bills.

In today's financial world, such a scenario seems crazy. One has to ask themselves if Bill and Martha need financial or psychiatric help, because despite the bills, the collection calls and the vialed threats, they just keep on spending money. But it turns out that Bill and Martha's problem is as much a financial one as a marital one. Bill (a Republican) keeps on buying cars every year (military spending), and Martha (a Democrat) has redecorated her kitchen for the 5th time in as many years (entitlements). The two can't ever agree on money (budget battles every year in Congress) each just keep on spending money hoping to blame the other when the sheriff arrives (bankruptcy) at the door to take their cars and house... with those pretty granite countertops Martha just put in. The kids (voters)? Like all kids they are clueless, but they have noted lately that "Mommy and Daddy always fight about money" (government shutdowns). The kids don't realize that they cannot take their toys with them to the homeless shelter when the Sheriff comes. Both Parents don't have the heart to tell them, but the "clueless" kids are starting to ask more pointed questions these days. Questions Mom and Dad should have asked themselves long before the racked up all that debt.

But Bill and Martha have another problem. The banks to whom they have been making payments have noticed that the money they are paying them with is counterfeit (Quantitative Easing). Bill and Martha are printing up money to pay their bills. The banks have turned this information to the other creditors (China, Japan, and other major Central Banks) and each now are considering reducing their credit line to bill and Martha but also taking other less pleasant action. Last week, Bill and Martha, finally agreed, after years of bickering to reduce the cable bill and get rid [of] the high end cable channels (last week's Budget deal). But each plans on continuing on with the same spending patterns in other areas with no change.[3]

Any person in the right mind will know that this financial situation is not sustainable for very long. Because of this big burden of sovereign debt, all the major economies must keep growing. Economic growth will drive increased use of energy, especially oil.

The next likely cause of the global financial system collapse is the sudden depletion of critical resources, such as oil. We shall see if oil has reached the peak oil status much talked about in recent years until the United States claimed to have an abundance of shale oil. (*Peak oil* refers to the time at which we reach the global maximum rate of oil production, which is followed by decades of declining rates of production.) At this point in writing, Bloomberg reported on May 22, 2014:

> The Energy Information Administration slashed its estimate of recoverable reserves from California's Monterey Shale by 96 percent, saying oil from the largest U.S. formation will be harder to extract than previously anticipated.

"Not all reserves are created equal," EIA Administrator Adam Sieminski told reporters at the Financial Times and Energy Intelligence Oil & Gas Summit in New York today. "It just turned out it's harder to frack that reserve and get it out of the ground."

The Monterey Shale is now estimated to hold 600 million barrels of recoverable oil, down from a 2012 projection of 13.7 billion barrels, John Staub, a liquid fuels analyst for the EIA, said in a phone interview.[4]

As I have shared in Chapter 2 that we are likely to fail to understand the exponential function, the fact remains that even if we discover oil, with the reserves doubling the current estimates, it can be depleted exponentially very fast. If the price of oil suddenly increases to an inflationary level, de-globalization can unravel very fast. It will be cheaper for the major economies to produce goods and services domestically than to outsource to low-wage emerging economies.

Due to oil's pivotal role as a transportation fuel and the key raw material for most consumer goods, the global economy can only grow if oil supply continues to grow. In order to keep producing more and more oil, you must keep discovering more and more. This is not possible. Presently there are over forty thousand oil wells around the world. One hundred or more giant oil wells, mostly situated in the Middle East, contribute about 65 percent of the current oil production capacity. Another four to five thousand oil wells contribute a further 30 percent. The rest of some thirty-five thousand oil wells make up the balance of only a few percent. These over one hundred giant oil wells are so large that they were all discovered by the 1960s. That implies future discovery of new oil wells is likely to be small oil wells with insignificant contribution to the production capacity.[5]

At the same time, the production capacity of the existing oil wells will decrease over time, as it will take more energy to pump up when the oil level in the well drops gradually.

The global peak for conventional oil sources has occurred in 2006, according to the International Energy Agency, requiring us to turn to unconventional sources, such as shale oil and oil sands.[6] These sources are expensive to exploit and will not last for very long.

Chapter 6

THE INSIGHT

This is now the second letter that I am writing to you, beloved. In both of them I am stirring up your sincere mind by way of reminder, that you should remember the predictions of the holy prophets and the commandment of the Lord and Savior through your apostles, knowing this first of all, that scoffers will come in the last days with scoffing, following their own sinful desires. They will say, "Where is the promise of his coming? For ever since the fathers fell asleep, all things are continuing as they were from the beginning of creation"....But do not overlook this one fact, beloved, that with the Lord one day is as a thousand years, and a thousand years as one day. **The Lord is not slow to fulfill his promise as some count slowness, but is patient toward you, not wishing that any should perish, but that all should reach repentance.** *But the day of the Lord will come like a thief, and then the heavens will pass away with a roar, and the heavenly bodies will be burned up and dissolved, and the earth and the works that are done on it will be exposed.*

—2 PETER 3:1–4, 8–10, NIV, EMPHASIS ADDED

I HAD BEEN SHARING in the regional pastoral conferences since 2011 about the coming global financial system collapse. Yet not only does the global economy continue to recover, but it has hit new records in the stock exchange indices around the world and industrial production.

The message I am sharing is getting stale. And the

urgency to prepare to face the coming collapse has waned. Is there anything that I have missed?

In the beginning of 2013 I prayed fervently for an answer from God as to whether or not I had misconstrued His message. Then came this insight, which I had really missed. In chapter 18 of the Book of Revelation, three groups of people will weep upon the demise of Babylon. They are the kings of the Earth (the governments), the merchants (the multinational companies and the small and medium enterprises), and those who make their living by the sea (the global seaports and the global shipping lines).[1] Some of these major seaports, like Hong Kong, Shanghai, and Singapore, are major financial hubs too.

In the 2008 financial tsunami, though the merchants and those who made their living by the sea did weep, the kings of the Earth did not. They were capable of mounting a rescue together, which they did. Today, the balance sheets of these major economies have been significantly impaired by this rescue effort. They will not have the means to mount another rescue in the future, when the crisis will be so much more severe than the last one.

The mother of all collapses did not happen in 2008, as the kings of the Earth did not weep then. In the next crisis, all three groups will finally weep and mourn at the demise of Babylon.

Given this revelation, I finally understood the link between the visions. The 9/11 terrorist attack was a judgment on the symbol of this western capitalistic system. The 2008 financial tsunami was a judgment on the system itself, but it did not result in the global collapse, as the kings of the Earth did not weep then. The next judgment will be the judgment that collapses the global financial system, which will lead to a new world order and a new world currency.

God is not slow to fulfill His promise. He is just patient toward us, hoping we will get out of Babylon quickly and escape the plagues of mourning, famine, and death.[2]

It is really sad that while we eventually knew the root cause of the 2008 crisis was greed among the financial elite in this Babylonian system, the current situation proves that we have not learned any lessons from the 2008 crisis. The same sin of greed and over-indulgence in physical pleasures in the globalized world today far exceeds the levels in 2008, which God detests.[3] By the time the next crisis happens, these sins will be heaped right up to heavens.[4]

Did God give other fellow brothers and sisters similar visions and insight into the coming financial system collapse and even the likely date? Will these judgments be seven years apart?

I happened to read of similar insights from authors like Jonathan Cahn and John Hagee in their respective books, *The Harbinger* and *Four Blood Moons*. I am now certain that this insight given by the Spirit of God in early 2013 completes the message that God had initially given me. The message is the coming fulfillment of the judgment mentioned in Revelation 18, with our gracious God being ever so patient and merciful in continuing to give repeated warnings through previous mini-judgments so that we can wake up and respond positively, coming out of Babylon before it is too late.

Chapter 7

THE PREPARATION

Then I heard another voice from heaven saying,
"Come out of her, my people, lest you take part
in her sins, lest you share in her plagues."

—REVELATION 18:4, NIV

N REVELATION 18:4, God exhorted His people to come out of Babylon and escape the plagues of His judgment, namely famine, mourning, and death.

How do we prepare to come out of Babylon?

The whole world seems to embrace western capitalism. Some countries in the world have tried other systems like communism and Islamic theocracy, but none seem to work well except the present capitalist system.

Do we sell everything and have nothing to do with the commercial world? Does it mean that we have to forsake all banking services and all aspects of life in this financial system?

Most economies in the current capitalist system run on debt. Consumer spending accounts for over 60 to 70 percent of total spending in these economies, and this spending is possible through consumer debt. Most of the production capacity expansion is only possible through debt in order to meet the demand of consumer spending. The major economies have to borrow to build infrastructure, to avail funds for production capacity expansion, and to fund important programs that will be productive in the long run. Financial institutions are in the business of marketing this debt. It can be said that we need a necessary evil like debt to oil the present economic system. Sadly, the major economies are borrowing irresponsibly to fund expenses that are not productive. Borrowing has to be controlled responsibly. There must be fiscal discipline. A common reason for amassing too much debt for the consumer is simple greed. We want more "things" than we can afford, so we accept servant status to the bank in order to enjoy now what we cannot afford to buy now.

It is sad that as much as the countries want their citizens to spend to oil the functioning of the economy, sometimes the oversight over the citizens, who are amassing too much debt, is not there.

We learned from Scripture that godly men like Daniel could still live and work in the pagan Babylonian empire and even hold high positions.[1] When godly leaders governed America, the enslaving power of debt was restrained, and the interests of the nation and its people were placed ahead of the interests of the merchants of the Earth. Only in recent decades, as Christianity waned as a force in western societies today, have these priorities been reversed.

God may not be asking us to get out of the actual system itself, like the examples mentioned above, but rather we are not to be contaminated by the values of the system. Daniel had remained faithful to God despite the politics and conspiracies in the pagan king's service. Despite the challenges faced in the building of the new American nation with the church separate from the state, the founding leaders wisely did not separate God from the state. They acknowledged God as the Source of their human rights, and they placed biblical morality directly into the founding documents and laws, though most of these laws have been repealed in recent years.[2]

I believe God exhorting us to come out of Babylon is to exhort us to come out of the worldly values today. We must not be weighed down in dissipation and be drunk in the maddening wine of debt.[3] Our slavery to debt is voluntary.

Nobody can force us to take on higher debt. So, it is our greed that cause us to be in such state of slavery. Living within our means is a prudent manner of coming out of the Babylonian financial system.

We must not put our trust in the good life as promised by this current Babylonian system, otherwise when God judges the system we are left feeling hopeless and mourn. Or we may be impoverished of food and lodging—literally—and be caught in the worst famine of our lives.

Do not be preoccupied with growing your money with financial products either. Imagine that you have yourself covered with all kinds of savings of fiat currency, and all these disappear with the collapse of the system. How will you feel when the hope you have in this system disappears? The citizens of Cyprus and Greece woke up one morning to find this a reality. Do not place your hope on perishable things but on the imperishable. The parable of the rich fool is a warning to us living in the present as well. We must not fill our barns with self instead of with God.

We cannot plan too much, leaving out trust in God, and we cannot afford *not* to plan either, putting God's warnings aside. We need wisdom and balance in the way we live today.

In chapter 11 of the Book of Acts, we learned that a prophet named Agabus went from Jerusalem to Antioch, and while there he predicted a famine over all the world. The brothers in Antioch determined, each according to his ability, to send relief to fellow brothers in Judea. Barnabas and Paul were tasked to send this relief to the leaders in Judea. Likewise, should the financial system collapse and famine be one of the plagues, the churches must rise up to help one another according to their ability. These churches should now prioritize their spending and save some "grain," or relief, for the coming famine, just like in the days of Joseph.

The church must meet often to spur each other toward love and good deeds and also to pray to escape the times. We will be more committed to each other as we meet and work together more often.[4] Each of us are given individual gifts, vocations, and skills by the same Spirit.[5] We are to use them for the glory of God in His kingdom, and all the more when the hard times are here.

Those with legal knowledge can help fellow brothers when they face unfair business practices and litigation. Those with biochemistry or agricultural knowledge can help to improve the yield of the farms of fellow brothers. Those with medical knowledge can help fellow brothers to have cost-effective medical care plans. Those with business knowledge can help fellow brothers who face cash flow problem during the hard times.

Let us be the faithful servant whom our Lord will commend when we provide food at the appointed time to fellow servants.[6] Let us be the sheep who do kind deeds to the least of our fellow brothers.[7]

Many authors have written about personal physical preparations to face economic collapse, like making the right investments, buying some silver and gold as part of the investment portfolio, or relocating to places with plenty of water and sunshine so that there is little or no reliance on fossil fuels. I will not delve into such preparations, as I believe God will generously grant each one of us wisdom as we ask from Him.

Let the local church pray often together so as not to be alarmed when the hard times are here, as the Spirit of Christ will be with us. Let us heed the warning from our Lord to guard against spiritual apostasy, inordinate fear over calamities, and persecution.[8] Let us endure to the very end. The Lord is good, and He is our refuge in times of trouble. He will care for us who trust in Him.[9]

All glory to Jesus Christ, our Lord! Let Him come soon!

NOTES

PREFACE

1. See 1 Corinthians 1:26–29.
2. See Ezekiel 16:49–50.
3. See Romans 1:24.
4. See 2 Chronicles 7:14.
5. See Hebrews 11:7.
6. See Luke 17:26–27.
7. See Revelation 18:4, 8.
8. Prasso Ministries, "Rising Unemployment Rate Forecasts Increased Suicide Among Protestant Christians," OregonFaithReport.com, accessed Aug. 13, 2009, at http://oregonfaithreport.com/2009/08/protestants-have-high-rate-of-suicide/.

CHAPTER 1

1. Nu Horizons Electronics Corp was delisted when the acquisition by Arrow Electronics Inc., a *Fortune* Global 500 company, was completed in 2011.
2. See the parable of the rich fool in Luke 12:16–21.
3. See Luke 4:18.
4. See the parable of the ten virgins in Matthew 25:1–13.
5. See Luke 14:25–33.
6. See Ezekiel 36:25–27; Luke 9:23–27.
7. See John 14:6.

CHAPTER 2

1. See Ezekiel 36:25–27.
2. See Colossians 1:19–22; Ephesians 2:12–22.
3. See Galatians 6:15; 1 Corinthians 7:19.
4. "Al Bartlett," *AlBartlett.org*, accessed July 27, 2014, at http://www.albartlett.org/.
5. Albert A. Bartlett, Robert G. Fuller, Vicki L. Plano Clark, John A. Rogers, *The Essential Exponential! For the Future of Our Planet* (Lincoln, NE: Center for Science, Mathematics, and Computer Education, University of Nebraska, 2004).
6. Dr. Chris Martenson, *The Crash Course*, Chapter 4, accessed August 1, 2014, at http://www.peakprosperity.com/crashcourse.
7. Todd Strandberg, "The Normalcy Bias and Bible Prophecy," *Bible Prophecy Blog*, accessed July 25, 2014, at http://www.

47

bibleprophecyblog.com/2011/01/normalcy-bias-and-bible-prophecy.
html.

CHAPTER 3

1. Anthony Ho, "The Coming Financial Tsunami," *Agora Antioch,* June 20, 2005, accessed July 25, 2014, at http://agora.antioch.com.sg/article.php?story=20050620140947376&query=financial%2Btsunami.

2. John Stuart Gladstone Wilson, "Bank: Historical Development," *Encyclopaedia Britannica Online,* accessed July 26, 2014, at http://global.britannica.com/EBchecked/topic/51892/bank/273030/Historical-development.

3. See Deuteronomy 15.

4. See Leviticus 25.

5. Susan C. Aro, "Tuba ordinance to institutionalize moral recovery program," *Philippine Information Agency,* November 2, 2012, accessed July 26, 2014, at http://car.pia.gov.ph/index.php?article=71351569842.

CHAPTER 4

1. John Stott, Ed., "LOP 21: Evangelism and Social Responsibility: An Evangelical Commitment," *Evangelism and Social Responsibility,* Lausanne Committee for World Evangelization and the World Evangelical Fellowship, Grand Rapids, MI, June 1982.

2. Hydraid™ bio-sand water filter manufactured by Triple Quest Inc. More information is available at http://www.triplequest.com.

CHAPTER 5

1. "Bretton Woods System," *Wikipedia,* accessed July 24, 2014, at http://en. wikipedia.org/wiki/Bretton_Woods_system.

2. Source: United States Government Accountability Office, http://www.gao.gov/assets/670/661234.pdf.

3. Mark Watson, *Watson's Web,* accessed July 26, 2014, at http://www.markswatson.com/index1-1-14.html.

4. Naureen S Malik and Zain Shauk, "EIA cuts Monterey Shale Estimates on Extraction Challenges," May 22, 2014, accessed July 26, 2014, at http://www.bloomberg.com/news/2014-05-21/eia-cuts-monterey-shale-estimates-on-extraction-challenges-1-.html.

5. "The Architecture of World Oil: An Elementary Update," lecture by Prof. Ferdinand E. Banks, Energy Studies Institute Seminar, November 2, 2011, National University of Singapore.

6. Dr. Faith Birol, interviewed in "Oil Crunch," ABC Television Network, *Catalyst*, April 28, 2011, accessed July 27, 2014, at http://www.abc.net.au/catalyst/stories/3201781.htm.

CHAPTER 6

1. See Revelation 18:9, 11, 17.
2. See Revelation 18:4, 8.
3. See Revelation 18:7.
4. See Revelation 18:5–6.

CHAPTER 7

1. See Daniel 2:48–49.
2. Francis A. Schaeffer, A Christian Manifesto (Wheaton, IL: Crossway, 2005), Chapter 2.
3. See Luke 21:34.
4. See Hebrews 10:24–25.
5. See 1 Corinthians 12:4–11.
6. See Matthew 24:44–46.
7. See Matthew 25:31–46.
8. See Luke 21:21–28.
9. See Nahum 1:7.

ABOUT THE AUTHOR

Anthony Ho was born and raised in Singapore. He graduated from Singapore Polytechnic with a technician diploma in engineering and with honors from the National University of Singapore with a Bachelor of Engineering. In his professional career he last held the position of president in a group of Asian subsidiaries of a NASDAQ-listed American company before quitting to wait upon the Lord's calling into ministry. He was an elder, minister, and pastor of three local churches from 2009 to 2014, and he is currently an itinerant pastor of Alfa Omega Ministry Indonesia based in Singapore.

Made in the USA
Las Vegas, NV
13 May 2023